MOVING

ALSO BY ELIZABETH GREENE

The Iron Shoes
We Who Can Fly: Poems, Essays and Memories in Honour of Adele Wiseman

MOVING

POEMS BY *Elizabeth Greene*

For Kerry,
Great seeing you at reunion —
You are someone who makes a
difference.
All good wishes,
Betsy
May 29, 2010

inanna poetry & fiction series

INANNA Publications and Education Inc.
Toronto, Canada

Canada Council for the Arts Conseil des Arts du Canada

ONTARIO ARTS COUNCIL
CONSEIL DES ARTS DE L'ONTARIO

The publisher gratefully acknowledges the support of the Canada Council for the Arts and the Ontario Arts Council for its publishing program.

The publisher is also grateful for the kind support received from an Anonymous Fund at The Calgary Foundation.

Library and Archives Canada Cataloguing in Publication

Greene, Elizabeth, 1943-
Moving : poems / by Elizabeth Greene.

(Inanna poetry and fiction series)
ISBN 978-1-926708-10-2

I. Title. II. Series: Inanna poetry and fiction series

PS8563.R41737M68 2010 C811'.54 C2010-902259-9

Cover design by Valerie Fullard

Printed and bound in Canada

Inanna Publications and Education Inc.
210 Founders College, York University
4700 Keele Street
Toronto, Ontario, Canada M3J 1P3
Telephone: (416) 736-5356 Fax (416) 736-5765
Email: inanna@yorku.ca Website: www.yorku.ca/inanna

For Alan
and everyone else who helped me move.

All of us trying to find our way back home.
—Gwendolyn MacEwen

Contents

Magic

Magic is imagination working together with dexterity,
... the heart working with the fingers to remind the head
how little it knows. —Adam Gopnik

In poetry, language is the tool
the deck of cards I watch you shuffle
flourishing the four aces or the two of
diamonds. The magic's in your hands, soft,
making the tricks look effortless,
fooling.
                    Red balls juggling in the air.
The juggler tosses, catches,
makes it look
                    easy. *Look, it's easy.*

I never have been deft
not with my hands
                    not even with my words
I cast my line,
haul boots from the depths.

No, if I have magic at all, it's not that, not tricks,
not spells. Memory maybe, or listening to
stars, or settling for the truth of old drowned boots.

Ghost Tree

Imaginary Friend

Imaginary Friend,
a channeller once told me you were real,
spoke in your voice of love we'd shared
through lifetimes. We'd walked, hand-in-hand
I imagine, by the Nile, by the Seine, in forests
under guardian trees, through gardens,
bending to greet the lilies and the roses.
                    Were you brown-haired,
green-eyed, dressed in white? At least once
we must have been girls together, waited
for love, grown through marriage and children,
soul twins.

Why didn't I find you in this life?
I gave my heart over and over to friends
who couldn't match you, couldn't last,
as we must have, through tragedy and sorrow,
couldn't speak heart's truth or
roll in silver laughter. Another life
maybe we'll meet. This life,
I'm on my own.

Imaginary Cities

Shangri-la, Atlantis, Lemuria,
Xanadu, Mu! Magic names – I say them
and their domes rise high,
my mind's eye flying far beyond my feet
to their streets, their stalls at the bazaar –
women walking with their children; men
talking God or politics; potters making jars
for olive oil or myrrh.

If I could go someplace enchanted,
I'd choose old Athens, study with Socrates,
old Rome, hear the poems of Ovid, Virgil,
Martial when they were new. Or Dante's Florence
or London when you might meet Virginia Woolf,
Ezra Pound, H. D. walking before breakfast
or Katherine Mansfield dancing to inner music.

Louis Kahn knew it: the right spaces make the spirit
soar. Piazzas, buildings flowing into heights,
markets abundant with pears and apples, olives,
dates –

I want a city where I can look for friends
linger over tea, buy cherries in summer, browse from
shop to shop, wonder at antique bronze and vases,

gorgeous silks, amethyst earrings, rosewood desks,
get lost in rows of oranges.

I want to wander fabled streets, each step taking me
through as many levels as Schliemann's Troy.
Present heaven, in those moments, sun on old stone.

Imaginary Music

Forget the madeleine: the most potent sensual jolt
in the first book of Marcel Proust's In Search of
Lost Time *is felt when Charles Swann falls under*
the spell of a "little phrase" in a violin sonata
by a provincial composer named Vinteuil.
—Alex Ross

Forty years later, I'm still looking
for Vinteuil's *petite phrase*,
that short run of notes Swann
hears and falls in love, finally,
with Odette. In Proust's world of
changing passions, shifting surfaces,
the *petite phrase* runs, underground
brook, surfacing with plash and rush,
then scrambling out of sight, like Odette,
more constant. Swann searches for
both, and so do we readers, even
after we've closed the last page of the
last long volume.
I thought
if I could find those notes, I'd find love,
like Swann, art like Marcel, but now
I know I must dive deep into
Imagination, feeling the thicknesses of water

as I descend, then emerge, gasping for air.
No heard music haunts me so much,
promises so much as those imaginary notes.

Unmysterious Origins

My origins aren't mysterious.
I know my birthplace and my hour,
my parents' names and something of their
stories, know my grandparents' names,
though three died before my birth.
Beyond that, there's a barrier, as if my
parents felt they could leave the past
behind, live in the present, new and fresh.
But how can you know what's in your veins
if you don't know the past?
Beyond the suburbs, beyond colourless
apartments, there are mysteries.

i Green Tree

We were Grünebaums – someone changed
the name a century ago before the First
World War. Assimilating. Who were those ancestors
long ago in Germany who lived with trees
in their names? And who
lopped them off? I carry them with me
like phantom limbs, clustered around
my extra "e."
One tree or a grove? Do I inherit
loneliness or company?

ii Shors

All Shors are related, my mother said.
She didn't say *One of the twelve tribes of Israel*

descended from Reuben. "Shor" means "ox."
She mentioned rabbis and scholars. She
didn't say a Shor wrote a version of *The Golem*,
ultimate story about letters and creation, about
a rabbi who made an almost-man of river clay
and water that had never known a vessel,
spoke incantations and holy words,
placed letters on the Golem's forehead,
maybe "*emet*" (truth) or the Holy Name,
brought him to life and instructed him:
fight the enemies of the Jews.
When the Golem ran amok,
the rabbi removed a letter,
turning "*emet*" into "*met*" (death).
A story about words breathing life,
and taking – holy words, making miracles.

I met my mother's uncle George and his wife Dotty once.
They lived deep in the country.
I remember trees, everything green.
Be careful of the poison ivy, someone said.

A deer, a fawn, ate from my hand.
Such a soft mouth, soft eyes. It could
eat poison ivy – *must have an iron stomach*
someone said. Its name: Deer Square.
I had to puzzle for years to understand that meant "dear deer."
Why didn't we ever go back?
Maybe my mother grew ashamed of me,
ashamed of herself.

iii "The Crack in the World"

When I saw the article by Thomas Shor,
"The Crack in the World,"
my heart leapt. Could this wanderer,
mystic searcher, *be related?*

The story carries me to Tibet:
hidden valley, secret door, a safe place,
a gate only opened by someone of unquestioned faith.
The lama: Tulshuk Lingpa, crazy treasure revealer,
was instructed in a dream, or several dreams, made notes
about the way to the gate, high on Mount Kachenjunga,
the rituals to appease the guardian spirits,
the time to go: October, 1962.
Three hundred followers
sold everything, never expected to return,
fled from massed soldiers to a cave at the top
of the world. Twenty waited for a month
as the sky closed down. They saw the gate –
they were that near –
but every time they started their approach,
the snow closed in, drove them back to shelter. They
waited day after day as the snow piled and the sky
flickered between blue and grey.
                                                    Finally
it cleared. The lama ventured out with his
consort and two holy men: Yashi to clear the way,
Lachung to hold the rear. They went down the slope
and started up. The weather held. But

just before they reached the notch, an avalanche
poured through the pass and buried them..
Lachung dug out and found
Yashi and the lady, badly hurt.

At the end of a trail of notes, he found the lama –
serene, cross-legged, dead beneath the snow,
as if his soul, at least, crossed the divide into
the secret world.

The gate still waits – *I could take you there* says
Yashi, *but what's the use without the lama?*

That longing for the hidden land, dream truer than life,
that clear vision of the sky the mind can fly in
after days of storm, that mystic nuttiness –

I began in certainty, grew
toward mystery.

Two Memories

The Cup

All of a sudden I know how to get there –
the gold-edged china cup glimmering on its hook
way high up, on the cupboard's second shelf.
I push over a chair, long stretch to the cupboard's ledge.
Then carefully, carefully up to the first shelf and then
the second, inching along. I can reach!! I can touch!!
Luminous porcelain cool to my fingers.
Then a scream –
                              my mother furious I'd climbed so high.
I drop the cup. It shatters. She snatches me down.
I don't die. But no more climbing.

The Piano

What I loved was not learning pieces
but playing out battles between low and high notes
over the keyboard. The divider started out at middle C,
my ear moved it down to
where the notes growled and menaced.
Low, high. Dark, light. It was never easy,
Still I knew even then at seven
even in spite of my nightmares of death camps
the dark may surge and bluster, even win for a while,
but at last the light overcomes the dark.

Moving

I hated to leave that house behind,
the Rose of Sharon tree outside my window
the blueberry bushes, sandbox, swings.
I was seven.
                    I hated to leave
the ghosts of my first cats – Smokey One,
Smokey Two, Grey Greene, Copper and Felina.
Five cats in five years, vanished. My mother
too afraid of death to mark their passing,
bury or mourn them.
                    I hated to leave my friends,
double-jointed Linda who could walk
on her hands; Valerie, who ate fish on Friday.
                    I didn't understand that
for my mother age seven meant tragedy,
the age her little brother died, hit by a car
nearly thirty years before, didn't understand
how she lived in fear.
                    She might have felt
disaster hovering, might have sensed it was time to move.
Closing day came in the midst of storms.
Never put off a closing, our lawyer said.
The sale went through. Next day, the roof blew off.

In our new house, the power failed.
We weren't at all sure about the furnace.
We stayed with a friend for a month.
I felt, at seven, the best of my life was over.

Nobody Home

After we moved, my mother
told me stories of
Nobody Home, invisible
rabbit who ate our tulips.
When the lady of the house
(my mother) came out and saw
the bitten leaves, she yelled,
Who ate my tulips?
And a small triumphant voice
floating from behind the weigelia,
Nobody Home!
No matter how she tried to trick him,
he was always brunched, invisible:
Peter Rabbit of the tulips.

I don't remember the tulips
in that garden.
I remember the bitten leaves,
the snapped-off heads.
(How did she know it wasn't squirrels?)

Nobody Home!

The Loneliness of the Long-Distance Searcher

My mother said, *You never asked a single question.*
But I did: *What is God? What's beyond the edges*
of the universe? Isn't nothing something?
My mother's answers only told me
you don't always find out what you want to know
by asking. You have to search, keep an eye out.
Eventually the answers will come to you. Or not.

My mother approved some things I came to love.
Cathedrals were spacious friends, each one a presence.
Medieval Latin was fine, so was Italian art.
Jung and tarot drove her wild.
Good thing she never knew about astrology, shamanic
healing, studies in Kabbalah.

She would have favoured my trip to Greece,
but not questing after mysteries,
not seeking forbidden knowledge
I gulped like water,
thirsty plant that I was.

Now I know these questions
were my inheritance from her ancestors,
Jewish mystics who climbed through the Kabbalah
tree, got to the top, glimpsed the edges of the
universe, the Ain Soph, the holy realm beyond

creation. I, watching, from a lower branch,
amazed, a little scared of heights they scaled.
That nothingness: yes, it's something.
Makes my mind spin. I'm still searching.
After sixty years, a little less lonely.

Ghost Tree

Even before I knew there was a ghost tree in my name,
I'd climb the willow next door,
gaze at the sky through its silky limbs,
press oak leaves like red stained glass into my books,
look at the sun glinting through maples,
lamplight turning leaves into disco dancers.
I'd lean against large trunks, feel trees growing,
            roots reaching deep into the earth,.

At nineteen, I'd go into cathedrals,
stone-sacred groves,
settle as I would under a tree.

When I'd go back to that small
close-walled apartment,
my mother would be waiting,
small dusty whirlwind,
all anger and grey hair.
Why didn't you call? There's
something terribly wrong with you.
You need help.

I didn't know then
illness was consuming her.
She was the one who needed help.

            At nineteen I spent a lot of time with trees.

The Diving Bell and the Butterfly

Eventually everyone loses everything.
—Edna Alford

i

Locked-in syndrome. We've all got it.
For years I couldn't leave the house.
First, my mother worried. Then, my son got scared.

But Jean-Do's locked-in syndrome, after a sudden stroke,
left his brain and one eye moving, that's all.
Those few moments, bleeding on the brain stem
brought him from life to a border land
at the edge
                        of the sea
                                                immobile.
He couldn't speak or turn his head,
just think and feel. His body there
but useless. With his one eye
blinking yes or no,
he wrote a book. *Bouleversant*
said one review ten days before he died.

ii

My mother at seventy-two,
tumour on her brainstem

started mumbling about warm chairs.
At the end, she could barely talk,
locked-in, managed *I love you. Is the baby*
all right? I sat with my son on my lap,
read nursery rhymes, tried to avoid
ones that talked of death.

My father, losing half himself,
acted as if she wasn't there –
How could he, so shy, not understand
that by speaking as if she couldn't hear,
he was being unkind
to silence.
Did my mother feel that? The diving bell,
the body, sinking, heavy, to the ocean floor;
the butterfly (mind, soul) flying free in sunshine
hovering above the flowers?

The Wolf

My mother kept nothing of her early life
no lamp or dish or locket of her mother's –
not even a photograph from her childhood home.
Reborn at seventeen, she tried to leave the memories
on the far side of a wall, buried in her mind.

A few half stories slipped through: endless fields of violets,
leads in high school plays, a longing for red hair
(hers was brown, incorrigibly curly). But the one story,
the one lurking like a wolf to gobble up
all that had happened since

was waiting for its chance and surfaced at the end:
her mother's seven-year illness, death when my
mother was fourteen; her young brother smashed by a car.
Her father, grandparents crumpled with grief,
sent my mother to the hospital to help him die.

So hard she tried to fend off memory
the wolf consumed her whole mind.
She lay silent, detached, surrounded by whiteness
in her hospital bed, spoke of love,
asked *Is the baby all right?* Sank out of life.

Leaving me blurred shadows, fragmentary clues.

My friends have long admired
the paintings she bought, the blue Venetian glass.

Deep in her brain the wolf fed
on the energy it took
to push away her story.

Pain Bodies

It is all a matter of translation.
I thought I read that in Auden's *The Dyer's Hand*,
I remember groggy July heat, my door shut
to keep my mother out – half a boundary –
her voice came through, but not
the rest of her.
                                        I was escaping into
Auden: *it is all a matter of translation:* lines on the
palm, words on the page, doors from outer to
inner, from words to wordless.
Did I escape deeper, into heat-soaked sleep, before or
after that passage, so un-Auden, settled in my brain?

I didn't know then about pain bodies,
inner entities. My mother's must have been
huge – inner self hurting, addicted to
suffering. Drama queen. Like physical bodies,
they hunger. The more you feed them, the more
they grow.
                                        My mother liked to play out
love scenes with me – part of my own pain body was
the thought I'd never know another love.

Not so long after, further north, in bracing autumn,
work and love finally starting to unfold,
I looked for that passage in *The Dyer's Hand*,
combed the pages over and over.

I could come back to unplucked four-leaf clovers –
why not to that cluster of healing words?
I could see them – but not on any page I turned.

I stared at my palm, wondering what it said,
at my handwriting with the small letters, low-crossed t's,
unable to translate myself to myself.

Transition, September, 1965

Riding in darkness
bus wheels whirring
no one lives here
not in this bleak dark stretch
of thruway
too much light to see stars
out of time out of space
just rolling rolling
where I know no one
where I've never been.
Behind me: a city I love
glittering, dangerous
the new around every corner.
Everyone thinks I should have stayed.
Behind me: a war only beginning to be
much talked of.
                                        They're buying barbed wire
from Australia my professor said,
Do you know what that means?
Concentration camps.
Our government!
                                        My father
believed the *New York Times.*
My mother didn't argue.
That should have told me
something was wrong.

Something *was* wrong:
for years my mother's words
(*you're too; you're not enough*)
shattered me, poured poison
in my ears.

I'm fleeing by night
unlikely refugee.

ii

Waking from fitful sleep
a different country –
flat, fertile giant squares,
fields, orchards,
late peaches, early apples.
No urban sprawl
not in 1965.

I can't believe how green
Toronto is. New York
was bleached with drought.
Black squirrels scamper
between large trees,
bushy tailed.
Victorian buildings settled
as if the last 60 years

had never happened.

I gave up friends,
the ease of being understood
back to childhood,
knowing where I belonged.

I crossed from the inside
to the margins.

Now even my spelling's
terminally split,
I teeter between honour
(honor), favourite
(favorite).

The years dissolved the poison in my ears.
I'm working on my heart.

Thresholds

Poised

Waking in darkness
full moon setting
serene
after its easy trip
across the sky
Orion hanging
over my porch
houses sleeping
old brick
old stone

Awaiting me,
Egypt and
a set of mysteries
half glimpsed before.
Nephthys, dark goddess,
the one I feel most drawn to
torn between her sister Isis
and her jealous husband Set.
Married badly, she
had to leave. Like me.
Dark, hidden.
Almost no one
knows her name.

Egypt! The guidebook says,
beware of bilharzia, malaria,
dysentery, scams.

Tourists are money on legs.
A trip full of perils
and wonder.

By next full moon,
I'll be back
shivering
under familiar stars.

Lost Luggage

Waking in Syracuse, I pull a card for the day: the Seven of Swords. What a card to start a journey! The man in his olive tunic stealing five swords, slipping away. No one watching – it's all so easy. My tarot teacher said once, *Sometimes you've got to be sneaky.* But what's sneaky about traveling all day and night, to New York and then to Cairo? My other cards show me hanging onto money, say this day will change me.

A beautiful November morning, the leaves still yellow, the air clear blue. I check my suitcase at the curb, in lots of time, write a postcard to my son, feel a wave of joy – I'm going!

Then down to the grunginess of travel, the constant announcements not to leave your luggage. The x ray spots an errant sandwich bag deep in my knapsack. (I'm amazed at this intense interest in my vitamins. I'm let off with a lecture to pack all my sandwich bags with suspect mouthwash, toothpaste, pills, close to the top).

In New York, I discover the meaning of the Seven of Swords: my bag was never loaded on the plane, mine and four others There's no luggage on the carousel. After a vacant while, the light stops blinking. Five of us swarm the baggage office, more or less politely. The man at the baggage office, unconcerned. Lost luggage happens all the time. So what if I'm going off to Cairo with the clothes I'm wearing and a knapsack, with two pairs of underwear, a sleeveless black t-shirt, my vitamins and Tarot cards. A nightshirt. A nail file but no scissors. My house keys. In my suitcase, a lavender veil meant for dancing in temples of Isis. Gone now. A white shawl, dedicate to Aphrodite. My bathing suit. Irreplaceable. Summer pants and skirts. A handful of Canadian coins. Should I just go home? I haven't traveled much for twenty years. How will I manage with no Arabic and no clothes?

Inanna lost her seven veils
descending to the underworld.
I've only lost a suitcase.
I hoist my knapsack, change terminals
for the plane to Cairo.

Thresholds

i

The first morning
before dawn
Mary talks about
fear –
            to be
initiate, you must
step forward, prepared
to lose, even your life.

I don't know if you need
to be so terrified as I was.
But as you leave your old lives,
you will lose things.

I'm ready, I think,
I've already lost
my luggage.

ii

We come to the Sphinx
under a dark blue sky
waning moon above
dark pyramids rising
from mist.

The Sphinx! I'd never
dreamed the darkness of its eyes
gazing through time.

We descend between its
paws, lean against the hieroglyphs
in stone, feel the magic.

We are protected,
instructed,
guided in meditation

and if we steal looks
from our inner worlds
we glimpse the sun's

first light slanting
on the pyramids.
Truly, we are folded
in Isis' wings.

iii

Leaving the Sphinx,
we see a plain of camels,
ooh and ah. From here,
they're pretty cute
chewing their cud
under woven blankets.

It's only when our guide

says, *The camels are for you*
that I feel terror.

We're supposed to RIDE
these creatures? Closer up
they look bad tempered,
have green mouths, unpleasant teeth,
bad breath.

Finally, after long paralysis,
I approach a camel
who gives a baleful look.
I'm pushed and pulled into the saddle.
The camel stands. I'm terrified,
and then we're rocking forward.
I have one picture of my grandparents
together. On camels, before the Sphinx,
maybe a hundred years ago. My grandfather
is fine; but now I understand my grandmother.
She wants to be safely *down; not here,*
not so far from New York and breakfast.
But then we're swaying past the pyramids
in the morning sun.
No, the camel's not happy; I should have
lost that weight; but now I feel the sheer joy
of being high, alive in morning air,
swinging through the edge of desert.
The Great Plain, the pyramids, the Sphinx
look different from this height.

No, I don't make it to laughter. And when the camel

starts to kneel to let me off, I'm sure I'm going
to slide right over his mean-tempered head.
And yes, I'm pulled undignified from the saddle.
But when I'm down, I feel the initiate rush
of being past the threshold, on the far side of fear.

Back at the hotel, there's coffee,
pomegranate juice, fresh fruit, eggs,
white linen tablecloths, the world's
most sumptuous breakfast.

The Horned Peaks of Parnassus

In sunlight, full of eagles,
in moonlight, full of stars.

Climbing Parnassus

Goat bells chinking far below,
saffron crocus singing to the sun,
I'm on a stretch of trail that goes straight up.
No wonder poets summoned Pegasus.
I'm on all fours, trying handholds, footholds
of unanchored stones or shallowrooted thorns.
How easy it would be to skitter
down thirty or forty feet,
let the mountain
stone me.
I hug the earth, suck
thorns from my thumbs, inch
step by step: it's not easy to reach
the Goddess.
Up here the world's all sky spilling
over mountain peaks. I can believe the Muses
dance here, sing by night to the stars.
I test each stone, each indent in the dry red soil,
urge my small magnetic force to bond
with the Mountain's, keep me going upward.
Try, slip, try, slip, try. Falling's
not an option.
                                        My hands, shoulders, hips, legs, feet
reach a stretch of steady trail. Upright,
I scan the valley, the goats below,
eye to eye with the peaks
circling the sky.

My knees shake as I walk.
Goddess, let me arrive.
Muses, even though I clamber, ungainly,
I've risked my bones to get here.
Let me bring back a handful of words
golden as crocuses.

The Cave

i

Underworld cathedral,
Even the lip of your entrance is
cool
respite from the hot October sun.
Guardian of the threshold:
massive Gaia stone
uncarved statue.
We bow, touch Her hem
at the brink of descent
into Her temple,
return
into our Mother.

ii

My eyes soar
to the vaulted roof –
even in this underworld
Greek light's
astounding clarity –

Below the ankles
my feet try not to slip
on Her bones.

A drop of water, Earth's milk

on my cheek,
the slippery stones
remind me this is a living cave.

I'm drawn to explore
crannies, hidden rooms,
though our guide warns
of danger in the edges,
dark uncharted cliffs
with deadly falls
beyond the reach of torchlight.

iii

We light our candles
in the stone circle that tells us
we are not the first or last to sit here.
Our sacred crystals,
my small owl
on the altar
call to Persephone,
but though this place is holy,
it only sings
her absence.

In the dark I descend
remember
all the lost daughters

carried off by men who were
unable to see beyond the
urges of a moment
filled with Plutonic lust
empty of love.

Then I feel absence after absence –
weep
for my own losses too.
The ritual is complete.

iv

That night in Delphi we learn
fighters in the Greek resistance
sat around the fireplace
where we had our altar
cooked, told stories, prayed
to our Mother for strength to keep the land
undefiled.
                    We also hear that just weeks before,
someone went into that cave alone,
explored the edges melted in darkness,
fell, never found.

Underworld seduction
descent without return.

Who Would You Be If You Were A Tree?

A graceful willow? Green-gold in spring,
weeping and growing in summer peace,
willow over water.

A maple? Sturdy, sometimes sugar sweet,
early leaves like tiny wrinkled parasols
lime green, red-tinged, growing into broad
flat canopies in summer.
Maples are good in each stage of life, raising their kids,
doing their jobs.
I grew up with one outside my window,
loved its flames in fall, its graceful shape in
winter. But to BE one? Could I ever
be so *regular*, even as a tree?

Fir? Spruce? Holly? Pine? I love their dryads,
especially at Christmas, but I don't want
to be that prickly, don't want to be such
a good sport in bitter winter.

Oak? Majestic, stained glass leaves in fall
to press in books, remember forever –
do oaks laugh?

I didn't know until I got to Karnak
in the golden dawn, came to Sekhmet's temple
stood beneath Hathor's ancient sycamore, a bodi tree,
tasted its unripe figs, felt its healing,

thought of its two thousand years of growing,
made my wish –
my ancestors must have sat under this tree
and talked of angels, light and dark, divinity, and
children.
More than the others, this tree welcomes
all comers to its sacred space,
blesses. I'd be a sycamore fig if
I were a tree.

Sand

I've never seen so much sand –
on the banks of the Nile
around the pyramids
on the roads.

From the train I see
sand out one window,
date palms out the other,
death on my left hand,
life on the other.

In Egypt sand is oblivion.
Clearing it reclaims history, form, event.
Uncovering the Sphinx, the pyramids,
enables memory.

Sandstone mountains rising from sand –
rusty, barren landscape of gods and pharaohs
just beyond, in sight of
the Nile's life-giving water.

The sand on beaches that ran between
my toes was just a pet, a purring summer cat
next to these Sekhmet-like devouring grains
that can bring a landscape back to zero.

We have snow that melts.
In Egypt they have sand that lasts.

Metal

Immortality here in desert country –
gold and silver set with lapis, coral,
engraved with letters, the power
of the word. Metal lamps soften
light into dancing beads flickering
tenderly over floors and walls,
gentle night after day's hot sun.

Here sand's the great leveller;
metal the great survivor,
embodiment of memory.
Sand ever shifting
metal steady beneath
carrying the words, the
craft of the dead.

In the Cairo Museum

Among the gold, carnelian, lapis,
imperishable casings of a mortal coil,
statues stride left foot forward
with eyes that gleam, still alive,
when beamed with light, waiting, like
animals in a zoo, for someone
to set them free, replace them
in tombs or temples, outside,
beneath the sky, near the flowing Nile
or desert sand, where they belong.

In the Cairo Museum I came across
my stepson in a past life, a statue of a sitting
scribe, necklace gone, neck cracked.
I recognized his nose, his lanky posture,
eyes dark as earth, waiting, for something,
they don't know what, long limbs
trained for ballet in this life. He had
a grand cross in his horoscope, which he
resolved by drinking, drugs,
happiest when out of this world.
The statue's mutilated, not broken,
a curse, not of obliteration, but of eternal pain.
They got that right, the old Egyptians –
we live beyond the single life.
What can you do with a curse like that?
Go back a thousand years and beg forgiveness?

What was the injury that caused the crack?
The secret's here, revenge of some old enemy –
so many lives lived wrapped in pain
like a mummy's shroud.

Grendel

Shadow lurker, earth stepper,
his home a cave piled
with bones and jewels.
Lived with his mother.
Happy enough until
he heard laughter rising in
new-built Heorot. Then he
was whelmed with
loneliness, last of his kind.
He heard it in the song, *seledreorig*,
wintercearig, wintersad,
homesick. He'd *been*
alone with the gannets' cries,
paddled the ice cold sea.

Drawn by the bright sounds,
he flung open the door,
stepped in the hall.
Eyes stared – warriors
reached for their swords.
Words rang; noise tangled.
Swords couldn't hurt him,
but the words! He didn't
belong, would always be
outside the songs.

He went back the next night

gliding in darkness
slipped inside the hall
soft with sleep breaths.
He felt the bodies, seized one,
bit, and as the blood dripped,
tasted the feast.
It wasn't what he'd wished for,
not first or second, third or fourth.

He darkened the Danes' feasts
for twelve long years
till Beowulf, bear's son,
fighting swordless, twisted
Grendel's arm off at the shoulder.
The monster lurched home.

The trail of blood
he left then was his own.

Grendel's Mother

When he came home, his arm gone, his shoulder
gushing blood, I wrapped the wound, took him in my arms,
cradled him as if he were a child again.
I said it would be all right, but I felt life draining.
I tried to rock him, soothe him, though
my spirit froze.

If only I'd made a happier home, maybe he'd never
have gone to the Danish hall. If we'd sung together,
would he have stayed? If there were others
like us, would he have kept away
from warrior feasts?
How much can a mother do?

Now I have two choices: vengeance and
death, or a coward's life –
enduring iron days in an empty cave,
mounds of bones, dry remains
of vanished dinners, piles of plunder,
jewels, plates, bright swords, singing victory
beyond the reach of memory.

As day dawned, my son was still.
Breath gone.
The cave shook with loss, I, wailing now,
no reason to stay silent.
I mourned, then chose:

revenge, no matter what the cost.
When night fell, I left my home behind,
retraced my son's last journey
to the raucous hall.

Beatrice

One day she appeared
in front of the Royal Bank
thin as a toothpick under faded
denim jeans and jacket
unruly chestnut hair
not shiny or dancing
but still taking in light from the sky.
Face like a bird's perching and startling
thin thin thin
ready to fly at a moment's notice.
Life raked her skin, left
broken veins in the hollows of her cheeks.
Her brown eyes had seen what they had seen
but still reached out to passersby,
not just for the coins.

She still cares for what she sees
as she stands or sits beside a building
where people get their money
and give her the crumbs –
and from these crumbs, she feeds the
birds. Sparrows eat from her long
thin hands or twitter beside her battered cap.
Sometimes she brings a flower; sometimes
a tattered doll.
                                    She says, she's going to
Vancouver where cold doesn't bite so deep
or last so long.

But year after year, she's there
feeding the sparrows, accepting our metal crumbs,
giving her blessings.

Then one day as the year turns toward
tulips and flowering crab, I realize she's
gone, has been gone for months.

Ingres' Comtesse d'Haussonville

Ice blue eyes, silk dress to match –
at nineteen I knew a heroine when I saw one.
Loved her cool querying gaze
so much mistress of herself
part butterfly, part Artemis.

As Ingres paints her, she's the room's
colour and soul, red flowers, red ribbon in her hair,
yellow shawl flung casually on the chair.

Opera glasses, calling cards suggest
her outer life, the hostess who gives
brilliant dinners, weaves connections
between politicians, writers. At her table,
a space for conversations *pleines d'esprit*,
civilized but cutting deep,
words that eddy into history.

The mirror behind reminds us there's
another side, an inner twin, the woman
who lost her much-loved sister, her first-
born son, kept going, loved or not,
happy or not, step by step, straight spine,
clear eyes. Wrote books, drew, composed,
found joy where she could.
Life of the mind the thread
that led through the labyrinth.

She knew M. Ingres
understood it all,
would keep her a heroine
as long as paint clings to canvas.

Neruda's Houses – Valparaiso

In Valparaiso I climb steep ship
stairways to a liminal
space

gazing from tree house
platforms
way out

to endless sky
and sea,

a space
where everything's reshuffled

so it's hard to tell where nature ends
and art begins,

where motion stops
and stillness
creeps in.

Take that sunset-orange cora cora bird
hung
within reach of
the dining room table –

it could almost sweep

out the window
swoop over the city.

A poet's home,
childlike, yet adult enough
for elaborate bars, hung with bottles –

Neruda's still here, drinking scotch
reading Baudelaire, Whitman, Lorca
in his cloud chair.

He might be smiling
at the crowds who
file through his rooms,

read the poem on his desk:

There is no money.
The house continues to rise.

In Neruda's houses,
                                        more is more
Mi deber es
        vivir
                morir

                                        vivir.

Matilde Urrutia's Shoes

In the Chinese laquered wardrobe
Matilde Urrutia's shoes, maybe
a dozen pairs, pink, pale green, but the
ones that touch me are the white ones
stained with climbing hilly streets,
or maybe from breakfast in the garden
as she stepped lightly through dewy grass to give
her heart to a hydrangea or a rose.
Jackie Kennedy shoes and
an ivory satin robe, unwrinkled as if
it had just come from Bergdorf's,
to put on after steamy evening showers
and shrug off as Neruda came
tenderly to bed.

Santiago

i

Secret Passage

Past narrow bar and hall
lined with watermelon paintings,
lush but bizarre,
in the small dining room, formal
enough for stately dinners but cozy
enough for riotous laughter.
Our guide, Alejandra, asks us what we think
might be in the third cupboard.
She opens it, shows us a false back,
a SECRET PASSAGE! Behind it,
a circular stairway leading up to light!
from public to private, political to
personal. Bores could be knocking
at the door and Neruda and Matilde
out of reach, in their aerie, drinking
white wine, looking over the city to the sea,
(*Lovers are the luckiest people in the world*
says Karen), leaving the mundane below
where it belongs, on the ground,
outside the door.

ii

The Library

Presided over by a Virgin Mary
with a broken nose.
                    She didn't save
the library when the crowd came
after the coup, after Allende's murder,
to sack the house. They broke the glasses,
dumped the books and papers in the library
outside on the ground, as if that would
bring back peace.
                    Neruda
wasn't there – he was at Isla Negra with Matilde.
That didn't save him. He died nine days after
the coup (*of a broken heart*, says Karen).

In the library today, small Kodak photos
of piles of books on the path outside
left to weather and ruin.
                    It's quiet now, late
summer afternoon, the house restored, grapes
ripening on the arbour in the courtyard.
Neruda's spirit lives here, but the drafts he
wrote here, the pages he read
          vanished
                    forever.

Isla Negra – Neruda's Sheep

Standing in this spacious study,
hand on the large serene wood desk
where Neruda wrote in his green ink –
was it ever littered with drafts? –
looking out at the ever-changing ocean
breaking over rocks and sand –
the room blessed by portraits of
Dante, Whitman, Poe –
you'd never know a sheep once
wandered here, in and out,
lifting its tail and leaving,
as Neruda said, a rosary of
brown beads on the polished floor.

Neruda knew
nature was not just in the rain
breaking on the windows, the sea
at the end of his view
constantly impelled toward shore,
but also in the mongoose who
lived with him in Ceylon, the badger
who shared his home in Mexico until
it bit the maid and left her sprawled
on the floor, bleeding from the neck.

We are made of the same stuff,
the same ebb and flow inspire us.

Maybe that's why Neruda's rooms,
like his poems, still breathe, still
make us spin and smile and dance.

Dreaming the Land

I smell the danger in the air
So close that I can taste it here
Coming from a few miles up the road.
—Terry Tufts

Well it's time to get together
Everyone who loves the earth
All those who want to save it
and all those who know its worth.
—Ellen Hamilton

My son and I drive north,
past country towns, general stores
calm houses built
to weather extreme storm and searing heat,
brick, stone, reflective windows,
dustings
of gingerbread trim.
Cows graze on sunbleached grass.
The land is breathing, as it always has.
We're driving to protest a mining stake
near Robertsville
north of Sharbot Lake,
to keep the land
drowsing beneath the seasons' turns.

ii

We know we're there when banners
blare from the gates:
Ardoch land in Ardoch hands
Ardoch Algonquin First Nations
No uranium!

A month ago a friend and I brought
boxes of juice, fruit, beans, corn, bread
tomatoes, rice. The gate was opened –
we drank coffee
at the edge of a makeshift village, long prefab
trailer, tents, men in camouflage, a fire.
A dark-eyed man, unhurried, took us aside, told
us the importance of water, land, the power
of the Mining Act:
mining companies can drain a lake,
poison a watershed, don't need to repair, restore, repay – and
it's all legal.
                    Today, the gates are guarded, locked.
We stay outside. Around us, untouched summer in
late morning light.
Wise old stones set among the grass.
Tough pines and spruce make living here
look easy.
                    A group of people sit under a tent,
talking softly, in for the long haul.

I feel too shy to greet them. We sit on bumpy stones;
unwrap our sandwiches. We eat. We leave.

iii

Over the weeks, as we return,
the sun, the sky, the trees
change from summer to the brink of fall.
We start to talk to others in the circle
outside the gate, share their food, their stories.
Some have been here in all weathers, will stay even
when the snow flies. Calm and resolved,
anger burning underneath like the earth's core.
Behind the fence, men in army greens
and women keep the fire going,
cook, wash, brew coffee, smudge –
smell of sweetgrass in the air,
singing chanting, drumming, talking, silence.
Telling the land we're here, we care.

iv

Two roads beckon:
guarding the earth, leaving it to
dream beneath the changing light,
or ripping, gouging, selling the ore,
leaving the spewed-out waste,
radioactive, to the guardians,
breaking the cycles, the water no longer
able to listen to the air or land.
After the first puncture, there's
no going back.

v

In town, in court,
the company requests
this injunction:
Anyone within two hundred meters of the gate
is trespassing, can be arrested.
The judge complies, without a murmur.
As winter comes, people are arrested –
former chief Bob Lovelace, Paula Sherman,
Chief Harold Perry, age seventy-eight,
with a heart condition,
settler Frank Morrison, tall, white-haired.
His crime: wanting to live on land that
wouldn't kill him. Still later, other settlers
are arrested, an old guitar maker,
slender women
whose lives speak peace.
The judge rules: the right to mine
trumps rights to clean air or water.
He sentences the chiefs to jail, slaps
large fines on the Ardoch,
lets the white settlers go.

vi

Bob Lovelace is in jail.
We gather in a parking lot
in Napanee to protest.
That's as close as we can get
to the Quinte Regional Detention Centre
where we'd thought Bob Lovelace was.

He isn't. He's been moved –
no one knows where.
February morning: no rain, no snow
no shadow.
A couple hundred of us
transform a stretch of
cement that could be anywhere
into a place of purpose.
Drumming.
Though all this
sounds the drumming.
Teenagers in skinny jeans,
mothers with their babies,
all arms and love, fathers with toddlers,
grandparents – some scrubbed,
some scruffy. Some carrying signs,
some just resolve.
We march down to the jail,
send our thoughts and light to
Bob, wherever he is.
We walk back, enormous drum
still beating.
            Whether anyone knows or not,
we have protested. The air has changed,
the sun glimmers through the clouds.

vii

I send Bob Lovelace books.
The Odyssey, two Harry Potters,
to the Lindsay Maximum Security
Super Jail. I send them Thursday.

They're back to me on Monday.
Jails must give mail wings.
Along with *razors, knives, booze and*
drugs, Polaroid photographs, photographs of
an explicit nature, photographs of a
correctional institution,
books (other) are not accepted.
The letter copied to I/M Lovelace,
Robert, OTIS # 1000724870
Unit 5F.

viii

Citizen's Inquiry: April 8.

Still cold. We gather
in a church basement,
hear speakers say:
Water is the blood of the earth.
We grow in water and
we ask for it before we die.

Shirts say,
Hell no, we won't glow. There's singing.
And there's drumming. The beat
of our Mother, the Earth.

ix

Unruly spring.
Rambunctious winds toss but
don't deflect the first small leaves

from their unfoldment
into green translucent hands exploring sky
and then real leaves. Magnolias burst
on the scene, no ingénue parts this year,
they arrive as stars. Tulips blossom
like balloons, red, lemon, orange, ivory, purple,
all over town winter gone,
tentative tender green now
singing with colour.
A court in Toronto rules:
Bob Lovelace is FREE!

Back at the Kingston courthouse,
we wait to hear about the fine.
The judge has arranged a tiny courtoom.
A few fit in. The rest of us lurk outside the window.
We're told we're making too much noise, though
no one moves to still the roaring lawn mover.
The judge rules: the fine is dropped; Bob Lovelace stays free.
After all, says the lawyer for the company,
our business is drilling holes, not courtroom fights.
They can still arrest us for being at the site.
But the land says, *Hell no, we are going to grow.*
The trees, the weeds, the grass
shooting up as if winter had never been.

x

Cool June.
We're hanging from the church balcony,
waiting for the concert. The air tingles.

Of course it starts with drumming.
There's Bob Lovelace in a red shirt with
his wife, you can only see the time in
prison from the glow around him.
Faces from Robertsville, from the courthouse,
from Napanee, from the Citizens' Inquiry,
all here now, lit with music. Bruce Cockburn,
guitar strings bright as comet tails: *stolen land*
that's all we've got. Stolen land and we're not done yet.
The church rocks, buzzes, rolls, we with it.

Bob Lovelace says, *I'd spend another hundred and three*
days in prison for another night like this.
We spill out into darkness
Inebriate of song, singing.

xi

Later we learn the company didn't wait
for mediation, consultation. That very June
they took core samples, lied that they had capped them.
No judge fined them for contempt.
Who can expect a business to be bound by law?
Profit is serious.
But a contractor in Chile says to me in January,
the money's gone. No one could borrow now
to start a mine.

Neglected House

It doesn't take much.
A few weeks of uncut grass,
flowers grown wild
weeds forcing their way
between paving stones
paths overgrown.
Then the chipped paint,
bleared windows,
sagging eavestroughs.
Spiderwebs on unswept porches.

So much of life is taking care,
polishing, cleaning, dealing with
dust, chaos' first frontier.
Bit by bit the house erodes.
Boundaries blur.
                                        Trees
grow up in front of windows,
skunks move
into the basement.

The house hangs on, dreaming of
years past, when its owner
pruned the pink roses,
cleaned the birdbath, trimmed the
candytuft, raised the son who
in his sixties doesn't want to sell

but doesn't want to spend enough
to make the house look loved.

You can see it pleading to passersby
Take me on, bring me back.

Burning House

Eight of trees – a woman, blonde
hair flying behind – fleeing
a burning house.

This is the break-up card.
When it chooses you, you know
it's time to leave.

Diane did it, came back one November
afternoon to get her contact lenses
and her daughter

looked at her books, clothes, pictures,
left as if she were going to the store.
The next day, the house burned down.

Diane and her daughter heartstoppingly safe,
beyond his reach.
Everything else, charred, ashen, ruined.

I did it, less heroically, no burning house,
but yes, a breaking marriage, anger
jangling through the rooms.

My childhood dream: to have the
loudest scream in the universe.
I finally tried it: that made him leave.

And now you, Miranda, don't hang on too long!
The house is burning, with anger, with
unkindness. The house says, *don't*
wait another minute! Find the door –
fly – blonde hair streaming behind you.

At the Chelsea Hotel

At the edge of literary history
in this room with grimy daylight,
at the bottom of a dry shaft,
thick mustard curtain hiding the unlocked
window just off the fire escape
no curtain on the bathroom window,
(not that anyone's lurking
in that uninviting niche).

The refrigerator's blazoned with a cheshire cat
male face, black sunglasses and a breezy pickup
smile – the sort of man I'd never spend the night with
even at nineteen—now, at sixty-six, I'm stuck with him.

This is a room where men bring one-night stands,
booze them, fuck them, drop them.

This room, in the same hotel where Dylan Thomas died,
giving up his green age too soon, where Sid Vicious
murdered Nancy Spungeon, where Leonard Cohen
and Allen Ginsberg tapped the vortex of ideas, desires,
climbed to the roof and higher, ecstatic with the view
or whatever elevator brought them there.

It's a language I don't speak.
I can't shut out the broken lamp, the lamp
about to break, the odd exploratory cockroach

in the tub, the smiling refrigerator's loud complaints,
the silvered radiator with its heartbreak crack
right down the middle, lamenting in the night.

It's not my language, but I begin to understand:
out of the ferment of bad art comes art.
Out of the fumbling and splitting of bad sex
comes myth.

Succulence

Succulent, luscious, scrumptious, sumptuous.
When I bought Sheila Lukins' *Ten*
on a mellow afternoon two years ago,
the words carried me back
to the mid-nineteen-eighties.
I read the *Silver Palate Good Times Cookbook*
year after year –
celebrating seasons' turning
with paeans to asparagus and chocolate,
ideas for party after party, good friends, laughter,
great food, *good times all the time.*
If I had the magic, I'd shimmy through the pages,
enter her dazzling world, guest at an herby clambake,
primavera wedding, fireside dinner.

Years before, I rode past the store, The Silver Palate,
on the crosstown bus, on my way to see
my mother lying in her hushed hospital bed,
recovering from a brain operation that Christmas;
dying – when the cells stole back
wasting her brain stem –
just before Easter.
I never had time to stop.
Illness has urgencies that can't be swerved.

From *Ten* I made the pot-roasted

chicken Santiago, shrimp curry, mango salsa,
pineapple ginger rice. Just reading the recipes
gave me hope – when I had the patience to cut
onions, carrots and potatoes fine, my guests
laughed contentment, the evening bathed in
glimmering party light.

Before I could try the
lamb tagine, I got an e-letter from Cookstr –
recipes in memory of Sheila Lukins. In memory of?
She'd died young, at sixty-six, brain tumour.
The viruses, eager and greedy,
recognizing the succulence of the imagination,
settling in to feast.

Endings (I)

Ah, C., don't make me write this story,
Tolstoy did it better, much better in
Anna Karenina; Jane Austen's chock-a-block
with worthless charmers – Willoughby, Wickham,
William Eliot. Guess she didn't much like the letter W.

Don't make me write this story with its glamour and
sordidness, the blasting dangerous love and later drifting
from place to place, rootless, a shadow of your former
self with only a demon lover for company.

Don't make me write this story.
Chaucer says of love: *an ounce of honey;*
a pound of gall.
Men like that may say they love you,
but they only love the high, being most
themselves by leaving themselves behind,
whooshing up and sliding down
(like a W). The glittering present isn't worth
the tawdry end.
Don't make me
write this story.

Endings (II)

If you want a happy ending, read a cookbook.
—Dennis O'Driscoll

In novels, stories, poems, you can tell the end,
in life, it's often hard to recognize
the moment you've lost a lover or a friend.

Earthquakes, tornadoes randomly upend
homes and families – news that horrifies –
in novels, stories, poems, you can tell the end.

Some people almost die, then breathe again.
Life gets another chance, unexpected prize.
We haven't lost, not yet, our love or friend.

Swann and Odette break, pull apart, return, then mend.
as two strings in cat's cradle harmonize.
In novels, stories, poems, you can tell the end.

You called, out of the blue, said you'd never speak to me again.
Five minutes on the phone. Stunned and surprised,
I scarcely understood I'd lost a friend.

Some quarrels aren't a breaking, but a bend.
Then a few unkind words turn love to ice.

In novels, stories, poems, you can tell the end.

In art, it's different. Writers sign what they intend.
Themes twist, pace changes, meanings crystallize.
In novels, stories, poems, you can tell the end
the moment someone's lost a love or friend.

Arrivals

Nothing Changed Much

Nothing changed much during those years
Tulips and daffodils shot up in spring
Seasons came and went under the stars.
Leaves fell in fall; in winter we made fires.

Tulips and daffodils shot up in spring
Every year you grew a bit despite your screams
Leaves fell in fall; in winter we made fires
What I longed for most: unbroken dreams.

Every year you grew a bit despite your screams
Litters of black kittens clawed the couch
Every night I longed for sleep, unbroken dreams.
I had a husband but I didn't see him much.

Litters of black kittens clawed the couch
We pruned the roses, planted herbs in spring
I had a husband, but I didn't see him much.
The paint flaked; the house slid toward ruin.

We pruned the roses, planted herbs in spring
You skated, played piano, lurched from year to year.
The paint flaked; the house slid toward ruin.
I dreamed my gravestone, woke up chilled with fear.

Seasons came and went under the stars.
Nothing changed much during those years.

Poets' Walk in Chile

Most of magic is looking and
listening, says Schmendrick, when
he's finally found his, in *The Last Unicorn*.
So here we are, walking along the edge of
vineyard, admiring the clusters of small green
grapes, hanging from generous vines,
scuffing up brown dust on this Tuesday morning.
If Van Gogh had been in Chile, he would have
painted these layers, above the road, the
swirly grapevines, then the pines with their spongy
needles, spiralling to the sky, top
branches bent in a permanent dance.
He might have caught the falcon
with its yellow breast and *timor mortis* beak,
its seeing-stone eyes piercing down forty feet
or more, noting us without interest.

Most of it is looking and listening –
the rabbit scat, the spiny little trees
on the bleached hillside, astringent eucalyptus –
small doors into the mysteries, into the poem.

Eleusis

This is the very spot
this cave, this entrance to
the underworld where
Persephone vanished, where
Demeter grieved.
Once Pluto carried her over
this threshold, no going back.
She was not just a fleeting interest,
but his bride. Somewhere in this
cave a border between surging life
and carven death, between time and
forever.
                    This is the spot
where Persephone emerged, returned
to tremulous Demeter, the spot where
for two thousand years the mystai
came to celebrate Eleusinian rites.
Once they descended and faced death,
their souls would never die a second time.

The site's in ruins now; cave entrance
blocked. We walked the sacred way
past dress and food stores, stopped
for traffic lights.

Still, there's no best before date
on reverence. We put our sacred

objects on the altar, invoke Demeter
and her daughter, ask them to bless
our journey, to let us be, even late,
initiate.

The sun slants from the west
as we leave Eleusis, continue
our pilgrim way. *Mystai, to the sea!*

Epidauros

Even though it's been in ruins
over a thousand years, healing's
still here, in the astringent, bracing air,
tall pines enclosing an enormous
grove. I can't see how far it stretches, but it
enclosed temples, residences, guest house for
pilgrims who came to heal, a school with
its fields (*mens sana in corpore sano*).
Healing's in the fragrance, in
unseen herbs, but also in the small sharp
knives and mysterious stones with holes
(maybe when they were hot, they drew infection?)
weapons to do battle with disease.
                                        If I lived here, I'd be an exorcist,
turning grey light to gold, troubles to resolves. I'd breakfast
on yogurt and honey, give healing in the day, talk shop over
lamb and rice.
I put my two-inch owl on my shoulder so he can see,
remind me if my memory fails. I keep him with me as I walk
back down the dusty road. This is the place
I most don't want to leave.

Phaistos

Everywhere we walk, they walked before.
They breathed in these mountains
rested in the the cave across the valley,
where Zeus was hid and nourished –
goat's milk from Amalthea,
honey from the bees.

At Phaistos, in Crete's south
sheltered from fierce northern rains,
sudden heat,
August in October.

The Phaistos disk was found here,
mystery picture writing
circling to a secret
at the centre.

Maybe a charm to stave
off invaders, men who
lived by war, served
an exacting father god,

believed in harsh order,
not in dancing over bull's horns
or the sacredness of Earth.
Maybe the Name of Her

who inspired these houses,
these streets, these festivals,
who gave grain, olives, rituals,
a thousand years of peace.

Or maybe it's prophecy:
the men in ships
who finally conquered
in the end.

Near Phaistos we find
a honeycomb of caves
carved in a seacliff
for Roman sarcophagi,

choose one for our final ritual,
smelling slightly
of death and cat pee.
It's an underworld experience, after all.

We place our sacred objects on the altar
my well-travelled owl,
Ellen's iron key,
Rachel's sacred knife.

Rachel guides our vision,

waves an ear of wheat,
and yes, I see her,
see Persephone,

giving her blessing,
showing the path,
from depth of descent
back up to light.

Persephone

On these dark days
when the last gold leaves
sputter on the ground,
I think of Persephone,
trim-ankled,
a flutter of white robe
scurrying in her wake,
as she glides away, always away.

For Demeter, her mother,
every moment an abyss
of loneliness.

Did Persephone miss Demeter
equally? Or did she start to feel
the lure of darkness,
turn toward Hades,
her smile enigmatic, radiant,
drawn by the desire of his iron heart?

Were there weatherless winter mornings
when they sat in state,
dark evenings when they danced by torchlight?

Descent, return
lover, mother
maiden become Queen

pomegranate at her breast,
ear of corn in her hand,
the mystery's core.

When you see her, you will know
you've passed the worst of darkness.
The only road home is through.

Walking the Labyrinth

True voyage is return.
—Ursula LeGuin

The most ritual way of going from A to B
Sure, you can cheat – step over the stone-lined
paths into the centre –
but the point is not arrival
at the speed of light.
The pacing is the process:
sending your soul out to
the sunlit pines, fluttering
silver-leaved aspens,
filling your cells with
clover-scented air
in this sacred grove.

We're tracing
a transposed rose window,
grass for pictures,
eyes in our feet.

Barry says, *Let some sorrow fall from you*
as you walk. I think of my son,
still finding his way at thirty-one.
How he'd love these clumps of mushrooms!
But as I step in toward centre, out toward edge,
I feel the rightness of the long way round.

Growth isn't always straight – what's wrong with
pacing every inch?

I'm at the centre now,
at the small stone altar,
with its lantern and offerings
pine cones, branches, pennies,
in the lap of trees.

When we've all arrived,
Barry reads his poem, then says
Sometimes things aren't what we expect.
Often the journey back is when the gift
is given most unexpectedly.

One by one we unravel the labyrinth,
Ruth, small and graceful, taking notes,
Cynthia, illumined with sunlight,
heart open to the sky,
Susan, summery in blue and white.
I know her poem will turn the whole thing inside out
and make me see it new – Barry, in his dragon shirt,
long fingers plucking lines from pine needles and air,
holding us in the moment he's created.

Then I know I'm inside poetry.
This is the way: circle round, don't hurry,
back and forth, let the poem take its time,
inhabit you.

À la recherche du temps perdu

I thought life was like that: dukes
and duchesses of Guermantes,
Swann's plucking catleya orchids
from Odette's Fortuny dress as they drove home,
the gleam in M. de Charlus' eye
as he noticed young Jupien.

Later my dreams were as small as
my son's day in school: would he
explode in anger so I'd have to bring him home?
I bribed him with hardware, locks
and doorbells. Somehow we stumbled
through. I started to breathe week by week.

Now my dreams are as high as
the sharp, carved-out Andes
under the dome of sky,
as wide as the sea stretching
way west, the view from
Neruda's house at Isla Negra,
waves crashing on the
wise worn rocks, as social
as dinner parties around tables set
with coloured wine glasses.

It wasn't what I'd expected,
but I'm still throwing my mind

up to the wind-scraped peaks,
still wishing on stars.

Old Cairo

After we heard the Sufi chanting to Allah
in the soaring mosque, we joined in.
Here, religions seem to blend,
lose their edges, oppositions.
After that, we went through the ancient door
into Old Cairo, tangle of tiny winding streets,
past small churches to the olden synagogue
where Pharoah's daughter found Moses in his basket,
close to the *mikveh*. Why had she come to bathe just then?
Was she instructed in a dream?

I walk in unseen footsteps of those well-worn stories,
imagine long-ago ancestors, nameless to me,
living in small houses, bringing up dark-eyed children
buying live chickens, sundrenched melons,
men, studying sacred texts, reading
Hermes Trismegistus in Egyptian, learning hieroglyphs,
puzzling out mysteries of creation, good and evil,
keeping the feasts, never thinking how far
descendants would stray from their faith –
would prefer trees, wind, goddesses to their one Lord.
I feel their presence, feel the traces of their beings
holding me here. I might have come to Egypt just for
these ancestors, just to walk these winding
crooked streets.

Hathor

I didn't know how much I'd missed her
before I came to her temple at Dendara,
rosy columns in the morning light –
cow-eared Hathor, descended from
the Milky Way, goddess of love and mothering,
song and dance, the sacred zodiac wheel.

Goddess for us all, not just size eight-
and-under film stars, models, singers who
make the pages of *People* with their hunky lovers.
She blesses each illumined heart.
Like the rich land around the Nile,
she'll console in tragedy,
but her realm is joy.
                                        Goddess without irony,
she is who she is, wife of Horus, mother of Ihy,
god of song.

Daimon est dea inversa: cows get a bad press
in the West, linking sacred and cow almost a joke
so I wasn't prepared for
golden Hathor with her crystal eyes,
mother, sister, lover, friend.
When the Pharaoh Hatshepsut fell in love with her architect,
She drank Hathor's milk, we know from the picture
at Deir el-Bahri.

In her small zodiac room

I see Nut holding up the sky.
I find the Lion, the Scales, the Maiden.
My sorrows, offerings, taken.
My body her temple. My destiny rewoven.
I didn't know I was so empty to be so full.

Philae

I didn't expect much. Up at four, dark boat ride, bumpy bus ride, waiting for a second boat, but then, with the first lightening of the sky, we're on a huge expanse of Nile, almost a sea, thanks to the Aswan Dam. Too early for even ripples over this vast water. We pass the island of Bija where Isis nursed Osiris back to life, and Set happened on him and killed him a second time. Osiris' thigh was buried near Philae. That's why Isis built her temple here.

We land, disembark, walk past closed souvenir stands to the temple, one of the rosy-columned ones, huge images of Isis, Osiris, Horus on the pylons. I've never felt Isis so close. Normandi gathers us in the inner sanctum, says, *Give me magic, the red knot of Isis where life and death meet.* Red magic runs in my veins. She lets us see that Isis is here, that in this temple Isis' earthly life meets her afterlife.

Ritual complete, we spill out toward the water, sit on a stone wall, ooh over an orange cat which greets each of us in turn. With me, he purrs, then bites. Rabies? I wonder. No, not here. I've been bitten by a holy cat of Isis. I'll be back. We wait for the sun to rise, to split Nut from Geb – and when the day's begun, the Nile rippling now, Le'ema dances, pulls the sacred from the air into her arms. She invites us all to join, and we do, bare feet on stone, in the first sunlight, in the borderline space where the Temple meets the Nile.

Then, because we're too early even for the guards, we get to enter the sacred precincts, climb ancient stairs with no railings to the roof, look out over the Nile, see other islands rising in the bright blue morning.

Isis, Osiris, Horus still live among these gentle stones in the long ages after their mortal lives and stories.

As we sail away, I know I'll return, maybe when my mortal life has slipped into afterlife. I'll arrive here by boat. Robed priests and priestesses will recognize me, greet me, pull me in.

Rereading *The Odyssey*

i

This time I see it's a poem about homes,
a paradox, a domestic epic about wanderings and arrivals
weathering sea and storms, recovering in the shelter
of spacious courts.
This time I'm delighted by ambrosial sandals,
purple mantles, well-made doors and well-planed thresholds,
chairs inlaid with ivory, water poured from golden pitchers
into silver bowls, feasts of endless meat and wine,
manners polished as the bowls and dishes,
winged words, no sludge on them, a style I've rarely seen
outside of books. Care in the smallest things.
Comfort in soul and heart as well as body.
Entering through the pages I forget about my own
dusting, vacuuming, dishes, about repairing the trim
or sweeping the porch. Falling through the spaces
between the letters and the words, I'm home.

ii

Telemachos begins to come of age by travelling
to the edges of his father's story:
to the courts of Nestor, Menelaus
kings back from war, their homes
restored to peace, sons and daughters
on the brink of marriage.
A small but stately journey

to get advice for dealing with
the storms of suitors
drinking, guffawing,
feasting on Odysseus' goats and sheep,
courting his wife
in his long absence.
returning
nothing.

iii

Rereading, I see the wine-dark Aegean, feel the wind.
I've climbed the slopes of Mount Parnassus
where Odysseus hunted the wild boar
that wounded him. Who would have
thought the scar, after twenty years of war
and wandering would say to his old nurse
Eurycleia, *Odysseus is home.*
I've seen Aegean weather change in instants
from calm to storm, seen waterspouts
Zeus poured from sky to sea.
I've walked on stony fertile soil
seen pomegranates, rosy as dawn, hanging
on unruffled trees, groves of olives,
glauques, like Athene's eyes,
behind them spiny mountains,
twin-peaked and winged
with their own sacred secrets.

iv

This time I see Cyclops' cave
not just as a story within a story
or an out of the frying pan into the fire
curse that dooms Odysseus to years more
wandering – I see it as a dingy bachelor pad,
piles of unwashed bones,
space shared with milling sheep
a huge stone for a lock, no one can move it
but the owner. Dinner provided by the
guests. I see my stacks of dishes,
unsorted papers, my windows that need cleaning.
Uncomfortable thought that when I leave this poem
I'll have to make my home a little more a court
a little less a cave. Small comfort that
I've never given anyone as guest-gift
the promise to eat him last.

v

After that, Odysseus visits
the enchanted halls of Circe and Calypso.
Invisible hands serve feasts
endless meat, sparkling wine,
clean the dishes and the sheets.
Circe's Hilton; Calypso's Mediterranean
Hideaway. Odysseus still traveling,
miles to go.

vi

This time I see Nausicaa as Joyce saw her,
long-limbed, young, a princess, but
a daughter first. Imagine a goddess saying
Go wash your dancing clothes!
And Nausicaa, blessed, listens,
comes to the shore with laundry
in time to encounter Odysseus,
naked, survivor of storm and raftwreck.
She tells him he's landed in Phaeacia
and leads him back to court,
to a welcome from her royal parents
who want nothing from their guest
but his story, arrange feasts and contests,
shower him with treasure and,
as is their age-old custom, offer him
safe escort back to Ithaca.
                                        It seems so simple.
Just get on a boat and go. It's all about
getting in position. When you're there, it
seems impossible that you spent ten years
being blown all around the sea, storms, shipwrecks, pitfalls.

An easy trip from Egypt due north to Odysseus' island.

vii

This time I feel the horror of
the lightning bolt that ruins the Phaeacian ship,
within sight of return, Neptune's last curse.

What justice in these deaths? All they wanted
was to help.
An ending too,
never again will the Phaeacians
escort strangers in need with such light hearts.
Nausicaa – she's bound to marry someone tall and kind.
How carefully she listened to Athene, how quickly
she took and washed the clothes – alacrity bodes well
for a good life.

viii

This time I understand
how hard Odysseus' homecoming,
how uncertain the ending.
I understand betrayal
from both sides,
how after twenty years
forgetting is as easy as remembering.

But for a reader, it's an easy choice.
I'm cheering for Penelope weaving,
reweaving, directing servants
seemingly serene in spite of
impending, unwanted second husband.
And Eumaeus, companioned by goats and swine,
keeping his memories heart-locked,
obeying when he must, but thinking darkly.
Laertes tending his figs and olives, more
like an aging hippie than a former king,
Eurycleia, remembering that scar.

They lived.The others died.

This time I notice the threshold
Odysseus planed himself,
the marriage bed he made,
care and cunning in all things
as much a hero in home and family
as in war.
                                        And when he's routed
the suitors and restored his home,
the poem ends. Why spin it out?
We've seen peace in the courts
of Nestor, Alcinoos, Menelaos.
We know what happens from
what came before

ix

I'm left thinking of home,
the ones I've made, the ones I've left
the one I live in bright with morning light
unheroic papers strewn on tables
and around my desk.
I'd never plane a threshold, lay a floor.
I'm wishing for
something of the seemliness of those
gracious courts filled with well-woven
purple mantles, ambrosial sandals,
roast lamb, retsina, honey from ecstatic bees,
kindness, guest-gifts, winged words.

My Father's Books

Gold-tooled, leather-bound,
endpapers marbled, hidden jewels –
ruby, emerald, sapphire, amethyst –
a nineteen-year-old's extravagance
but a promise too that, no matter what
life brought, he'd never forget the joy
of reading: Molière, Racine, Corneille,
Rabelais.
When he opened them,
did he see himself at nineteen crossing
Harvard Yard, the joy of mind leaping
to the sky? Or in his rooms, reading
till the windows turned blue, then dark
with night?
Or were they reminders
of his father's death, the money gone?

Still, angels always bless the unexpected.
My father kept that promise to himself,
read French until the end, wrote French
verse in alexandrines, signed his poems
Edvert.

Ninety years later, the books are in my
study, on the top shelf, next to my Pléiade
Proust, smiling at my son's photographs
on the walls, half-written poems on my floor.

Laundry

I dreamed:
suddenly everyone was writing
about laundry.
I saw a whole shelf, maybe twenty, books.
Joanne Page and P. K. Page
had done a slender perfect
volume, glosas and sestinas
hung with pink and purple shirts,
blue and khaki pants, flowing
skirts recalling lunch on patios
talking poetry and aprons
(also hanging on the line).
Each sock, each towel a page
of the symphonies of our lives,
a triumph of cleanliness over grime.
I saw clothes tumbling in dryers
scrambling round and round like
apprentice gymnasts or financiers.

As long as there's laundry, our lives
are turning, the clothes and cloths
we choose to wrap our days.

I wake, the other laundry books unread,
glean my sheets for dreams, strip them
off the bed, time to wash the sleep out,
return them clean, slip back another night
for other books.

Sudoku

for Cynthia French

I do it too, Cynthia,
even buy the paper for it
and don't read the news –
especially when I don't want
to face the outside world:
when I was trying to sell my house,
living with fake plants,
wrestling white coverlets over all
the beds for showings, ripping them off
when viewers had gone so that cats
wouldn't shed on them –
again when I was moving
oppressed by the thought of packing
the whole ten rooms, basement, attic,
shed in five weeks,
couldn't decide whether to do the books
first or the china or the garden tools.
I never did transplant the lemon lilies.
Or now, when the painters aren't arriving
to put the storms back and I'm cleaning
off the paint spots with my fingernails.
That's when I turn to Sudoku
where all I'm thinking is eighty-one small squares,

numbers from one to nine, where things fit,
or they don't – there's something about
beaming in laser-like on the blanks in rows
that snaps my mind into focus – takes me deeper,
almost into trance – into that deep pool at the bottom
of the well, wordless, where all things of the mind
begin.

Wires of Necessity

Strung tight on wires of necessity, I cared
for my son, husband, students, last of all the house.

It didn't look like prison, but I struggled
to get out the door. High ceilings, well-proportioned
windows, elegant, even when the wallpaper scuffed,
the paint chipped, the carpet frayed –
consolation in confinement.
The house should have made us leave, but kept me and my son.
After George left, we painted, gardened, got water damage
repaired. Step by step, my days enlarged: coffee
downtown; days in Toronto. I learned to heal;
my tears (mostly) dried.
We redid the third floor, sold, left that house behind.

Now I float down the steps, fling open my arms.
World, here I am! I walk by the lake,
blow dandelion fuzz. Ducks swim, butterflies
flit in the silk sunlight of a new-born day.
At the Sleepless Goat, I drink peppermint tea.
My horoscope says a wish might come true.
At home the cats fizz with purring.
At night I'm bathed in moonshine,
feel the wires stretch me to the stars.

Grey

All spring my horoscope's been saying
The door is open; you can leave your cell
behind. Or will you find it easier
to stay confined?

Horoscopes!
Obscure as Delphic Oracles! Should I
hop the next plane for Thailand or Vancouver?
Walk daily in rainforests, breathe in
the breath of trees till I see
everything that lives is holy?

Maybe it means I can leave grey
behind – those narrow years when
no doors opened, when I couldn't
see around the fog I lived in.
I'd be walking, working, but
I never got beyond the grey.

Now I can lose myself in foxgloves,
wild roses, peonies. A cell's a subtle
thing – a veil with you everywhere
blocking light, until you tear the fabric,
step out into unmediated air, listen
to the trees' green words, I
like a leaf shot through
with golden light.

Notes

Epigraph: "All of us trying to find our way back home" is from Gwendolyn MacEwen's "The Wai Mah Café."

Magic: Adam Gopnik's article, "The Real Work: Modern Magic and the Meaning of Life," appeared in *The New Yorker.*

Imaginary Music: Alex Ross' article, "Imaginary Concerts," appeared in *The New Yorker.*

Unmysterious Origins: Thomas K. Shor kindly replied to my querying email that we are probably not related (he certainly convinced me). His riveting article, "The Crack in the World," appeared in *Parabola.*

The Diving Bell and the Butterfly: Jean-Dominique Bauby wrote this book about his months of locked-in syndrome. He dictated by blinking his left eyelid to indicate letters.The book took ten months to write and was published March 6, 1997, three days before he died of pneumonia. The film (2007) includes the review, which Bauby received ten days before he died (in 1997).

Lost Luggage: the Seven of Swords is from the Rider-Waite Tarot deck (and corresponds to the seven of spades in playing cards).

Grendel: *seledreorig* (Anglo-Saxon): sad for want of a hall, homesick; *wintercearig* (Anglo-Saxon): winter sad

Santiago: *mi deber es vivir, morir, vivir:* I need to live, die, live (Pablo Neruda).

Dreaming the Land: Thanks to Terry Tufts for permission to use the lines from his great song "A Brighter Shade of Green" as the first epigraph to this poem. Thanks to Ellen Hamilton for permission to use the lines from her song "The Hunter" as the second epigraph.

Succulence: *good times, all the time* is on the back cover of *The Silver Palate Good Times Cookbook.*

Burning House: The Eight of Trees in Shining Tribe Tarot corresponds to the Eight of Wands in traditional Tarot and the eight of clubs in playing cards.

Poets' Walk in Chile: *timor mortis* – fear of death

Old Cairo: *mikveh*: ritual bath

Hathor: *Daimon est dea inversa.* A daimon (demon) is a goddess in reverse. This is an adaptation of W. B. Yeats' Golden Dawn name (*Daimon est deus inversus* or DEDI).

Hatshepsut was the only female pharaoh. She ruled from about 1473 -1458 BCE. She did fall in love with her architect Senenmut who designed her temple at Deir el-Bahri.

Nut: the Egyptian sky goddess, usually depicted in a downward dog pose holding up the sky. Geb is the Egyptian earth god.

The Lion, the Scales, the Maiden: Leo, Libra, Virgo

I didn't know I was so empty to be so full: This comes from Peter S. Beagle's novel, *The Last Unicorn*.

Several of these poems have been published previously.

"Imaginary Cities," "Metal," and "Old Cairo" appeared in *Free-Fall*.

"Moving" has been accepted for *Untying the Apron*, edited by Lorri Neilsen Glenn.

"The Wolf" was published in *The Antigonish Review*.

"Transition" appeared in *Crossing Lines: Poets Who Came to Canada in the Vietnam War Era*, edited by Allan Briesmaster and Steven Michael Berzensky (2008).

"Persephone" was first published in *Arms Like Ladders: The Eloquent She*, edited by Katerina Fretwell (2007).

"Imaginary Lover," "Matilde Urrutia's Shoes," "Beatrice," "Nothing Changed Much," and "Burning House" all appeared in the *Queen's Feminist Review*.

Thanks to the editors of these publications.

Acknowledgements

My resolution at the beginning of this millennium was to learn from the best, and the good influences and teaching of several master spirits helped shape this book and increase its reach.

Many thanks to my tarot teachers Mary Greer and Rachel Pollack, who first taught me at the Omega Institute in 2000 and 2001 and subsequently at workshops in Toronto organized by James Wells.

And thanks to Sharon Olds for two poetry workshops at the Omega Institute in 2003 and 2005. Sometimes days can be intense as years.

Rachel Pollack led an unforgettable trip to Greece in 2006. Rachel's power and presence, her knowledge of ritual and landscape, her sense of the sacred, her storytelling and humour all made the journey irreplaceable. Rachel's Shining Tribe Tarot was a companion through that trip and through much of the past decade, and her Eight of Trees is the inspiration for the poem "Burning House."

Ellen Lorenzi-Prince, a member of the Greek group, led us in a wonderful Drawing Down the Moon meditation at Nauplium. Her interest in solving the puzzle of the Phaistos disk stayed with me as I wrote the poem. Thanks, Ellen, also for your reading of many of the Greek poems.

Mary Greer sent me the oracle from Gwendolyn MacEwen which appears as the epigraph to this book. Once I received it, poems began to cluster around it. Mary was one of four inspirational leaders on a trip to Egypt in 2007. The words about initiation in "Thresholds" are hers. Thanks to the other leaders of the trip—Normandi Ellis, whose profound understanding of ancient Egyptian spirituality and whose wonderful writing transformed us; Gloria Taylor Brown, and Nicki Scully, of Shamanic Journeys Limited, who organized both Greek and Egyptian trips with incredible expertise, led us in initiatory rituals and created space for growth and healing.

Christine Irving was a cherished companion on the Egypt trip and a valued reader and correspondent in the months that followed.

The horoscopes referred to in these poems were all taken from Jonathan Cainer's website. "Imaginary Cities" was inspired by one of Jonathan Cainer's "Thoughts for the Day."

Thanks to Terry Tufts and Ellen Hamilton for permission to use words from their great songs as epigraphs to "Dreaming the Land."

Thanks to Bruce Cockburn and his management for permission to use excerpts from "Stolen Land," written by Bruce Cockburn ©1986 Golden Mountain Music Corp. Used by permission.

Enormous gratitude to Barry Dempster for leading an amazing poetry workshop in Chile, which was at once challenging, supportive and encouraging. Thanks, Barry, for lending us your eyes and helping us to see through our own. Thanks also to the other members of the circle especially to Susan Siddeley who organized the workshop. and, with her husband Gordon, welcomed us in their Chile home Los Parronales and managed to collect us all into a van for trips to the Neruda houses, in spite of our tendencies to wander off incorrigibly in all directions.

Thanks to Ruth Roach Pierson, who led me to Chile and who set us all such a great example with her devotion to poetry and her exceptional ability to revise so that her poems climbed new heights with every draft. Cynthia French and Carol Gall kept the circle going with their sharing and reading of full moon poems after we got home. Many of the poems in this book have benefited from their meticulous but generous readings.

Thanks to Barry and Karen Dempster for hosting the Chile reunion that led to "Walking the Labyrinth."

Closer to home, thanks to friends who are so important in my dailiness: Valerie Ashford, Carolyn Boyce, Heather Buchan, Kellye Crockett, Tara Kainer, Margaret Little, Elva McGaughey, Laurie Lewis, and to other members of the Kingston writing community. And thanks to long-distance friends Mary Lou Dickinson, who has shared my writing life since 1992, and Caroline Miller in Victoria.

Special thanks to Helen Humphreys whose suggestions for deleting weak poems and weak lines made this book much stronger and whose advice on rearranging the manuscript was (as usual) excellent and much appreciated. Thanks, Helen, for your fine reading and your friendship.

And to Joanne Page for initiating me into the mysteries of turning a poetry manuscript into a book and for her extraordinarily careful reading. The book as a whole and the poems in it are sharper and cleaner for her Banff-in-Barriefield editing.

Thanks to my editor, Luciana Ricciutelli, at Inanna Publications for her belief in the book and for her work in seeing it through press.

For me, home depends on my son Alan and our cats Binah, Shekinah, and Juniper. This book wouldn't be possible without them.

Photo: Kyla Raymond

Elizabeth Greene's first collection of poems, *The Iron Shoes*, was published in 2007. Her poetry has appeared in the *Queen's Feminist Review*, *The Antigonish Review* and *FreeFall* and has been anthologized in *Crossing Lines: Poets Who Came to Canada in the Vietnam War Era* (2008) and in *Arms Like Ladders: The Eloquent She* (2007) as well as in two anthologies she has edited: *Kingston Poets' Gallery* (2006) and *Common Magic: The Book of the New* (edited with Danielle Gugler) (2008). She edited (and contributed to) *We Who Can Fly: Poems, Essays and Memories in Honour of Adele Wiseman* (1997), which won the Betty and Morris Aaron Jewish Book Award Prize for Best Scholarship on a Canadian Subject (1998). She lives in Kingston.